HOUSTON '74

TELEPHONE PIONEERS OF AMERICA

TEXAS

TEXAS

A PICTURE TOUR

INTRODUCTION BY

LON TINKLE

EDITED BY

NORMAN KOTKER

CHARLES SCRIBNER'S SONS   NEW YORK

PICTURE CREDITS

Printed in Japan
Library of Congress Catalog Card Number 73–5198
SBN 684–13415–2

3   5   7   9   11   13   15   17   19   X/C   20   18   16   14   12   10   8   6   4   2

CONTENTS

INTRODUCTION BY LON TINKLE:
REFLECTIONS ON THE TEXAS LEGEND   7

A HISTORICAL PORTFOLIO:
THE CREATION OF TEXAS   29

A PICTURE TOUR   47

Title page: A field of bluebonnets
Left: Hereford cattle by a windmill

REFLECTIONS ON THE TEXAS LEGEND

By Lon Tinkle

There is a Texas character, a Texas caricature, a Texas myth, a Texas mystique, a Texas legend, a Texas tradition—and then there is a Texas reality. The latter is not easy to pin down. Since it includes a large mix of the myth and the mystique, of the legend and the tradition, of self-mockery as well as braggadocio, it is not susceptible to precise definition. But most Texans and outsiders sense and recognize this reality, as they recognize a friend, an acquaintance, or any vital living thing to which we give a name. The name Texas does stand for some kind of reality that is both like and unlike other realities that flavor our ideas.

Texans themselves, with an almost fanatical streak of loyalty, push hard for the belief that Texans and Texas are more "unlike" than "like." They insist on identifying Texas as somehow unique, original, different. It has an identity of its own so special that few other states of the nation claim such separateness. The chief rival at the moment is California, whose "uniqueness" is not simply colorful and dramatic but evangelical and prophetic.

Opposite: The Alamo

California is the new way of life, the theater on whose stage the life-style of post-industrial society is being rehearsed, maybe perfected. Texas could not claim to be an advance herald of this affluent society that is creating a new morality, a new sensibility, and a new vision of human happiness. California has annexed the future; Texas is possessed by the past. But, though different, each state has its own mystique. This is strange, inasmuch as both now have as many residents who are new, and therefore still outlanders, as they have natives. Like religious converts, these new-comers to the faith are often the most ardent, the true believers. The important thing about this vast flow of population into Texas and California since World War II lies in the fact that despite all this new "mix" of life-styles or traditions or customs, the living reality evoked by the words "Texas" or "California" is still unified. It suggests a totality.

So, at least, Texas proclaimed to the world when in 1968 the state celebrated, at the HemisFair in San Antonio, the 150th anniversary of its successful war of independence from Mexico. The theme of this world's fair was that "Texas Is a Confluence of Cultures." Ah, but not your ordinary confluence, a *different* confluence.

Texas's images are, with one exception, symbols of raw, uncultivated nature: first of all the cactus plant ready to claw with its thorns, the inevitable cattle skull, sticking out over the covering of dust storm dunes, the cowboy on his mustang pony, the battle-destroyed shrine of the Alamo, the Franciscan mission that is remembered in history as a fortress—and when the great gusher at Spindletop erupted, an oil derrick.

The images that flood the mind when anybody says Texas are, for native and outsider alike, images of the constant struggle between Man and Nature for mastery over each other. Cat-claw, wild mustangs, cow skull, oil pump.

These differing images symbolize the unconscious pieties which Texas like all communities secretly observes. For the Texan, the key "piety" is courage. Survival here has always been a challenge, not an inheritance or a natural blessing. The Texan's pride centers in his own endurance, not in his creation of a culture. His pride (when it is pride and not vanity) springs from his capacity to master nature, not from his capacity to harmonize with it.

For most people, the sense of time is more significant than the sense of place. Geography is less important than ideas and customs. It is otherwise, up till recently at least, with Texans. They are enormously aware of the role in their lives of place: land, or place, that has underground the golden wealth of oil, land that can accommodate ten million head of cattle, black waxy land that used to yield, as it may again when rehabilitated, the finest cotton ever grown in the world. Place for the Texan translates into space, the thing he's got the most of, and the thing that tests him the most. How appropriate that Texas, or at least Houston, should be the Space Center of the nation, the home of NASA, now re-christened the Lyndon Baines Johnson Space Center.

You almost *have* to think big when you live in a state that measures its east-west and north-south axes in terms of about a thousand miles each. These are boundaries as great as those of many nations, and larger than many of the most famous nations in history. Before the days of easy and swift transportation, most Texans dealing with their government had to travel, on horseback, from "sunup to sundown" to reach the county seat. Distance, usually a vacant distance, shaped the imaginations of the early-day Texans.

Distance is usually accompanied by loneliness. Although many idyllic landscape spots exist in Texas, most of the land is so flat and treeless and underwatered in the long periods of drought, that any Texan having to drive several hundred miles is certain to traverse roads where the horizon seems steadily to suggest the rim of the world, just where its round edges curve over into nothingness, where space comes to an end and the void begins. A physical tremor comes over the body; your nerves feel the pull of endless space where there will never be a final containing and harmonizing horizon. Weaker people are seized with terror and want to turn back to the comforts of community; the rugged persevere and stake their claims on the distances, as ranches, as oil holdings, as plantations. Courage, again, is the human trait most typical of Texans.

The history of Texas is full of heroes. The Texas Pantheon features the leaders of the 1836 War of Independence against Mexico, when such figures as Davy Crockett, Jim Bowie, and Sam Houston redeemed with great gestures lives that had sunk from national distinction to drunken and defeated obscurity; it includes lesser-known men of the Revolution of greatly varied temperaments, the gentlemanly and plucky Stephen F. Austin, the fiery redhead and heartsick lawyer William Barrett Travis, Travis' loyal compatriot and fellow-lawyer James Butler Bonham, and on through scores of names immortalized in the naming of Texas towns and counties.

Their memory is also immortalized in the Texas history textbooks that all students of the state are required to study in the secondary schools. Thus, even outsiders who move into the state—as when, say, Chance-Vought Aircraft moved from Hartford, Connecticut, to Arlington, Texas—are infected by the contagion of hero-worship in Texas. On vacations or at weekends, throngs of youngsters and their parents flock to the San Jacinto Battlefield and Museum near Houston, to the Alamo in San Antonio, to Goliad and Washington-on-the-Brazos, and to other historical spots in the state, the car licenses revealing a muster of numerous out-of-state plates, presumably of. new settlers in Texas as well as transient tourists. The public schools are named after the heroes of the Texas Revolution; so are the streets in many Texas towns and cities, as in Dallas, Houston, and San Antonio; the big banks of the big cities display murals in their lobbies celebrating the battles of the Texas Revolution; even some of the newest and fanciest hotels call their assembly rooms after Travis, Austin, Houston, or the second president of the Texas Republic, Mirabeau Buonaparte Lamar. With such a name, how could the man have failed to be a hero? With such ever-present reminders of past Texan glory, how can the schoolchildren of Texas fail to long for personal distinction and the desire to have their names carved on public buildings and perpetlated in a dozen other ways?

Outsiders who mock Texas for its primitiveness and its self-assertion, its bragging and boasting, forget that back of this offensive self-congratulation there burns the flame of a very vital belief in the old code of honor, even of *noblesse oblige*.

If the latter phrase makes you smile, applied surprisingly to a thoroughly unaristocratic tradition, you must remember that when Texas won its independence from Mexico and existed for ten years as a Republic (1836–1846) before annexation, it sent ambassadors abroad, had foreign legations on its own soil (the old French Legation is a show place in Austin, the state capital), and was courted by a number of European nations. In the effort to win colonists in their new republic mostly inhabited by Indians and bisons, the Republic of Texas advertised its favorable land grants heavily in Europe. The most beloved, perhaps, of the varied geographical units of Texas, LBJ's "Hill Country" west of Austin, was largely colonized by liberty-loving German artisans and scholars, led to the Promised Land by the Prince von Sohms-Braunfels himself. Followers of French socialist philosopher, Charles Fourier, made several settlements in Texas, under the leadership of such famous names in French socialist thought as Victor Considerant and Etienne Cabet. A distinguished Polish settlement was established at Panna Maria. In a beautiful but generally ignored area of central Texas, fanning out from Meridian, Norse settlers founded a dozen hamlets and villages that to this day keep their mother tongue and habits as do the Germans in the Hill Country.

When you recall that the oldest of the "big cities" of the state, San Antonio, was personally guided in its earliest destinies by the Marques de Aguayo, and that its first large consignment of settlers sent overseas by the Royal House of Spain consisted of families whose heads were designated "hidalgos" and given noblemen's privileges, you begin to see the justice of HemisFair 1968's claim to represent a "Confluence of Cultures." And of the mingled streams that encouraged in Texas a profound respect for a man's personal code of honor.

Perhaps related to this is the Texan habit of bestowing the supremely aristocratic word of rank, "king," on men who distinguish themselves in the state's three most decisive economic

A prickly-pear cactus leaf

The flat and seemingly endless high plains north of Lubbock

resources: cotton, cattle, and oil. "King Cotton" is not a Texas coinage, but "cotton king" probably is. The state's most distinguished historian to date, Walter Prescott Webb, popularized reference to cattle spreads as "cattle kingdoms." (Pleasantly, the most famous ranch in the world, by the accident of cognomen, is the King Ranch in South Texas.) The urge to royalty perseveres. Men who once were known as petroleum pioneers are now more chicly celebrated as "petroleum princes." An old Texas anecdote, still secretly cherished in many a native heart, makes this hunger for distinction and fame clear. A young Texan lad was rebuked by his father for a breach of good manners: "Son," admonished the elder, "don't never ask a man again where he's from. If he's from Texas, he'll tell you. If he ain't, there's no need to embarrass him."

And, to end this point about the Texan's peculiar pride, the best study of the state made in our time, John Bainbridge's amiably ironic "The Super-Americans," attributes the maintenance of the Texas tradition to the very rich, who take delight in all the outward and ostentatiously visible signs of pride, from privately owned Lear jets for the men to Neiman-Marcus ermine and mink for the ladies. However obvious the display, the unconscious psychological sanction for it—both for the successful and for those he impresses—is the fact that he has emerged from a testing, from a trial of strength, as a victor. The "killer instinct" or the "championship syndrome" or the badge of being "really tough, but really tough"— these are the proud insignia of so many distinguished Texas men, distinguished on a national scale as well as regional.

Is this "champion complex" the lesson of Texas' proud and particular history? Hardly. Another Texas story may indicate the difference. It concerns a youth from Tennessee who decided to join the parade of Tennesseeans heading out to help Texas, from Sam Houston (former governor of Tennessee) and Davy Crockett (former Congressman from Tennessee) on down. The young fellow astonished his neighbors when he rode from farm to farm to tell his friends goodbye. He shifted his Tennessee rifle to his left hand as he held out his right for his compatriots to shake. He wasn't old enough to be of much help, so every neighbor put the same question: "But, Jim, what on earth are you riding off to Texas fer?" His reply, delivered with angry rebuke: "Why, I'm going off to fight for my freedom."

He was right in his impulse. It was for freedom, shared freedom, it was for independence, mutually respected independence, the "Texicans" were fighting for. Greed, too, or at least land hunger played its part. The Anglo-Americans who came first to Spanish-held Texas and then to Mexican-owned Texas were lured not only by virgin land and open space and independence but by free land and free space and the obvious chance of sometimes being a law unto oneself. But most of them were partially, at least, also motivated by idealism and the wish to help turn America into the "Garden of the World." In a crisis, they were not only companionable and convivial men (drinking was very heavy), they were also chivalric men, bred on heroic oral literature, laced with the influence of the novels of Sir Walter Scott. They did not believe in turning back. Davy Crockett's famous motto, which used to be plastered on classroom walls all over the state, was "Be sure you're right, then go ahead."

The early history of Texas may be quickly capsuled. Although Texas was discovered by Spanish conquistadores as early as 1519 (when Cortés was just discovering Mexico), nobody wanted the place till three centuries later. Two of the most famous names in colonial history explored the state not long after the first arrival in 1519, Cabeza de Vaca and Coronado. Neither found in Texas or the American Southwest the gold and silver that made Cortés's conquest of Mexico so spellbinding. Spain established a claim to Texas, but left the land to the Indians and to the herds of buffalo.

After Coronado's futile search for the Seven Cities of Cibola (whose existence had been reported in Mexico City by Cabeza de Vaca), many other *entradas* were dispatched from the capital of New Spain into Texas. They discovered nothing of interest. The action was in New Mexico; the first Texas

Overleaf: North of Big Bend National Park—a barbed wire fence, a gate, and Nine Point Mesa in the background.

13

settlements were along the Rio Grande near El Paso del Norte on the way to Santa Fe and Taos.

France, greedy for Spain's endless seams of gold and silver in Mexico, wanted Texas as a point of departure. LaSalle in 1685, whether by mistake in looking for the mouth of the Mississippi or, as is often thought, by calculated plan, landed near Corpus Christi, Texas, a colony of about 500 Frenchmen. This was disaster. He was killed by rebels amongst his own men, the colonists could not survive the hardships, and after five years the surviving few were victims of the cannibalistic Karankaway Indians.

Word of the French attempt reached the Viceroy in Mexico City. He knew Spain must hold its claim to Texas as a buffer state to keep at a suitable distance the Indians, the French, the envious.

So, for the next century Texas was simply a pawn, of no value in itself, contested for by the French and the Spanish. France attempted no more colonizations; Spain did, but nobody in his right mind wanted to leave the magnificent Central Plateau of Mexico for the wilds of Indian-held Texas. A few hamlets were founded, with the accompanying missionary fathers and soldier guards. The missions were to Christianize the Indians and to make them Spanish nationals, who would then hold the province for the glory of Spain.

The chief settlement was near the beautiful springs at San Antonio. When at last the Anglos in their westward movement reached Texas, around 1820, San Antonio had a population of perhaps two or three thousand. From a Spanish settlement it became a Mexican town when rebel Mexico won its independence from Spain in 1821, a revolution modeled on the United States' struggle for independence from England. Mexico invited the Anglo-Americans into Texas; Mexico still wanted it colonized as a buffer state between the rich Central Plateau and the marauding American Indians. The Anglo-Americans responded to the invitation with swift eagerness. Fifteen years after the Mexican program of colonization was in effect, nearly 30,000 Anglos had settled in, swearing allegiance to the Mexican government and to the Catholic faith. In exchange, they got incredibly large allotments of land. In 1836, there were around 5,000 Mexican nationals in Texas; the newcomers numbered

Eagle Mountain in West Texas's Hudspeth County, more than 7,000 feet high

close to 35,000. There were no churches, or only very few, where they could practice the Catholic faith they had accepted. The Mexican Republic to which they had vowed loyalty had been suppressed by President-General Antonio Lopez de Santa Anna and replaced by a tyrannical dictatorship. The Anglos, now known as Texans or Texians, had pledged allegiance to Santa Anna's Republic of 1824 and its Constitution modeled closely upon that of the United States.

Several provinces in Mexico rebelled against Santa Anna's replacement of the Republic by a dictatorship; these rebellions were ruthlessly quelled. When the Texans, who had many other grievances against the Mexican government because of tax impositions and neglect, also rebelled, Santa Anna set out to exterminate them. He brought into Texas, in a war that lasted about six months, troops that numbered close to 7,000 men. The Texans, who made their first stand at the old mission of the Alamo in San Antonio, had there only 180 or so men. At Goliad, eighty miles east of San Antonio, there were another 500, mostly young volunteers from the southern states who had come out to join kin or for the sheer adventure of it, and there were perhaps another 500 or so being organized by the commander-in-chief of the Texas army, General Sam Houston, who was a very close friend of President Andrew Jackson and whose mission in Texas was often thought to be a secret between himself and his illustrious friend in the White House.

The Texans, against overwhelming odds, withstood Santa Anna for thirteen days at the Alamo. Their last-ditch stand, a deliberate choice of holding out until death to gain time for their compatriots, allowed Houston enough breathing space to organize and recruit an army of defense. This army, six weeks later, destroyed Santa Anna's at San Jacinto and held him hostage to arrange a treaty for Texan independence.

Texas existed for ten years as an independent Republic, before her wish for annexation to the United States was finally honored. When admitted, Texas had a history of her own, a war of independence, monumental debts, a roster of tribal heroes, and the right—if she ever chose to exercise it—to split her vast area into five states. It was a privileged entrance into the family, despite the abolitionists' fierce opposition to taking in another "southern" state. Texans have never forgotten that

The ghost town of Terlingua, near Big Bend National Park, once a mercury mining center

they came into the union as a separate nation or Republic, with its unique privileges and its own revolutionary war—and with a dowry, so to say, of a quarter of the land in the entire nation. For as a direct result of the annexation, the United States was able to add to its territory the entire region stretching from Texas to the Pacific.

These self-evident truths are belabored in the state's textbooks, in the required courses in Texas history, in the newspaper editorials, in the self-congratulatory meetings of thousands of Texas clubs of every kind, study clubs, luncheon clubs, business clubs, and so on.

When news of the death of President Lyndon Baines Johnson filled the papers, magazines, and TV screens, one phrase occurred over and over: "LBJ will be buried beside his beloved Pedernales." There is no doubt that LBJ loved this river, as he loved the Texas Hill Country where his ranch is located. He came back to it because, as J. Frank Dobie said, "Nature puts something into man he needs." He came back to it for strength and succor. And the Hill Country is no doubt the favorite region in Texas for the natives. The quality of light there is transparent; the sun really shines golden, endowing often a succession of blue-gold, blonde sumptuous days with a quivering and haunting magic. Like many another oasis, so to say, in the nation, it is a country of sky, silence, solitude, and space. Above all, and again, one notes the importance to Texans of this sense of space. It is the innate poetry of their landscape, a landscape often dull and bare for immense stretches—till you look to the sky. But even these spiritless stretches come to life under the magic of spring, when the burgeoning, lustfully greening earth smells of the rich soils with their promise of harvest. Even these dull stretches speak out their loveliness as they lie under the glorious skies of October.

But it is a hard land to love if you are not born there. It is a capricious land, or as one native writer calls it, "a bitterly beautiful land." The seasons commingle as though by whim. Often Thanksgiving and Christmas and New Year's Day family celebrations enjoy either a late autumn mellowness and mildness or an early, deceptive springlike langour. The day before may have been freezing; the next day, if you insist on burning ceremonial logs in the fireplace, you'll have to open the doors. The countryside that you cursed for its bleakness in February is soon enamelled with the stunningly beautiful and varied Texas wild flowers. The summer days that wither you with heat when you venture outdoors also yield material delights that reconcile you to the hot season: the best tomatoes in the world, really acidulous tomatoes with true savor, all the "fixings" for the marvelous gumbos appropriated from Creole Louisiana, including superlative oysters, and crab and shrimp unrivalled by other waters; the best watermelons and the best cantaloupes you can find anywhere (and of course the incomparable "ruby-red" Texas grapefruit in its season); corn which when roasted and seasoned and drenched in melted butter, salted and peppered, will reconcile anyone to all the faults of Texas; the peaches from the Hill Country, the German sausages, the barbecued meats; the famous Texas beers; and, as crescendo, that greatest of all Texas culinary delights, true and honest chili.

Now, to the confusion and amazement of most Texans, outsiders are insensitive to these benedictions and blessings.

Overleaf: Ponies on a ranch in Kerr County, in the hill country of central Texas

Dime Box, Lee County, east of Austin, on a branch line of the Southern Pacific Railroad

Whenever LBJ's sudden trips home from the White House required the transporting of the Washington newspapers corps to the Hill Country, the boredom with the countryside and the indifference of these outlanders was such a shock that for once reporters made as much news, locally, as the President. Those purple hills we natives think of as mountains were belittled as mere mounds; the tonic air and the shimmering light went unbreathed or unseen, or so it seemed; the ever-changing vistas featuring the magnificent live oak trees, green the year round, and the outcroppings of lovely limestone rocks and slabs, were no treat at all. Amends were made. The staffs were quartered in Austin, our sparkling jewel of an up-and-down sylvan city rimmed by hills that remind Europeans of Rapallo; but the newsmen still missed the charms of a real metropolis. Next, they were quartered in nearby San Antonio, only twenty miles farther from the LBJ ranch than Austin, but even here, in Texas' most Mediterranean and most cosmopolitan city, the expected euphoria did not prevail. "The eyes of Texas" had no charm for these visitors if ever they even looked into them. As so often, Texas was saddened by the reactions it provokes in non-natives.

But this is not always true, not at least in the case of Europeans. Somewhere it ought to be on the record that Texas has long had an unexpected appeal for visitors from abroad. The most enthusiastic "discoverer" of Texas since World War II was the writer-painter Ludwig Bemelmans, who was astounded at a dozen things he never expected to find in a state so mocked by its fellow-states. Even the landscape, about which even most Texans are characteristically modest, bowled over Bemelmans, and he had a really mystic experience in the Big Bend National Park, that treasure of mostly unknown beauty shared by Texas and Mexico along the Rio Grande in the western part of the state. Many Texans can quote to you by heart what Bemelmans wrote about the Big Bend:

In a lifetime spent in traveling, here I came upon the greatest wonder. The mantle of God touches you; it is what Beethoven reached for in music; it is panorama without beginning or end. . . . It will make you breathe deeply whenever you think of it, for you have inhaled eternity.

As a footnote, one might mention swiftly that T. S. Eliot, just after marrying Valerie Fleming in 1958, came on a "honeymoon trip" to Texas because Valerie wanted to see it, and he savored his sojourn so greatly that he was said to have worn his ten-gallon Stetson, the inevitable gift of his hosts, in London in preference to any other head-gear. And that Thomas Mann in 1939, before settling in California, pondered staying in Texas at the beautiful estate of British portrait painter Douglas Chandor in Weatherford, Texas, whose gardens are internationally famous. As another footnote, one may notice that three of the most famous European women of the century maintain homes in Texas, Pola Negri in San Antonio, Lily Pons and Greer Garson in Dallas. Texas has no better propagandist than Lily Pons. On the other hand, everybody knows the comment of General Sheridan: "If I owned both Hell and Texas, I'd rent out Texas and live in Hell!"

Other strands are stitched into the complex fabric of Texan reality. The spirit of the frontier still lingers here, as does the influence, very strong until World War II, of fundamentalist religion, chiefly Protestant, which filled the state's major political offices with pillars of the Baptist faith; it used to be said that no one could be elected governor of Texas without being a Baptist. Controlling vote in the Texas legislature rested with the rural representatives even after half the state's population lived in the four biggest cities, giving a continuing agrarian cast to the tone of the government, although reforms are now correcting this situation. The economically privileged areas have dominated the state though their power has been countered somewhat since irrigation and technology have made formerly waterless West Texas a great cotton center, even as its role as ranching country is being contested by East Texas which is turning its cotton lands into cattle kingdoms. The damming up of rivers and streams and the construction, under Federally-funded programs, of an immense number of lakes, large and small, as a part of the flood-control program has turned habitually thirsty Texas soil into a water wonderland, at least in comparison with former days.

But another reality for Texans has no doubt been the often savage, and often deserved, mockery and low estimation of Texas by the rest of the nation. Our political and other scandals are truly of "Texas-size." When scandals occur, the rest of the nation slaps its thighs and guffaws. Oh, those poor Texans! It is all part of the primitive and immature ways of the adolescent of the national family, who is taking forever to grow up. When will Texas join the rest of the union? outsiders ask. Does there exist one single "quiet Texan," one single "couth Texan"? And so, Texans, with their childlike, if not childish, impishness and love of playfulness, answer back, "Never!"

Despite this rather churlish expectation that if anything can go wrong in Texas it will, Texas continues to enlist national interest. Texas is a state to watch, it's where a good piece of the action is. It is somehow "charismatic." Part of this lure comes from the zest and gusto with which Texas still struggles its way up from the frontier. In many Texans now in power in various fields in the state, the frontier remains a shaping childhood memory and influence. This is true, for example, of the two most prominent Texans in national government of this century, Lyndon Baines Johnson and John F. Connally. They came from a part of Texas where, in their boyhoods, "the pavement ended." Both had to struggle against poverty, both responded to the frontier challenge with Texas-size ambition and drive. Meantime, both felt that their lives were emblematic: if they could make it, as the saying goes, so could other young Americans who were willing to spend the same energy, the same dauntlessness, the same extrovert cheerfulness, perhaps, and the same hope for glory.

Their kind of exuberant drive still motivates Texas men of achievement in various fields, and notably in the urge to fill in swiftly the gap that separates Texas college education from that of the "top ten" universities in the nation. The hunger for cultural betterment in Texas is very real; the amount of money poured into Texas schools, symphonies, art museums, civic operas and ballets, and other cultural enterprises is staggering. Great fortunes have given great benefactions. The most recent, and perhaps the most stunning, is the new Kimbell Art Museum of Fort Worth, the state's fourth largest city.

When the Kimbell Museum had its opening in October, 1972, after six years of planning, it spurred national "rave" notices. "Breath-taking," said *Newsweek* of the architectural gem that the eminent architect Louis Kahn had designed and of the $30 million collection that the museum director—imported from Los Angeles—had put together in a six-year formative period. To establish the museum, a Fort Worth capitalist, Richard J. Kimbell, had left his home city a legacy of $100 million.

True, it's all imported: architect Kahn, director Brown, and the Picassos and Bellinis and Tintorettos and Matisses. But when one considers how often European museum collections represent the loot of conquest, one might exculpate Texas in this case. The Kimbell Museum is only one of a dozen instances of Texas' cultural yearning. It is noteworthy that in the same Fort Worth cultural complex there are two other important museums: The Amon Carter Museum of Western Art (a sterling building of Texas limestone designed by Philip Johnson) rich in Remingtons and Russells, and the Fort Worth Museum of Modern Art, rich in Rodin sculptures and in Picassos.

For most Texans, the frontier remains a powerful push, a potent memory data-bank from the past, but the pull of the future is as strong. Fort Worth still likes to call itself "Cowtown," though its stockyards and meat-packing plants are far less important now than in the early days. Fort Worth also likes to advertise itself as the spot "Where the West begins." Most Southwesterners agree, but its rival twin city of Dallas (a half-hour drive away) can no longer accurately invoke the comment it used to add to Fort Worth's claim: "Where the West begins —and civilization ends."

In fact, "the pull of the future" is so powerful as to cause

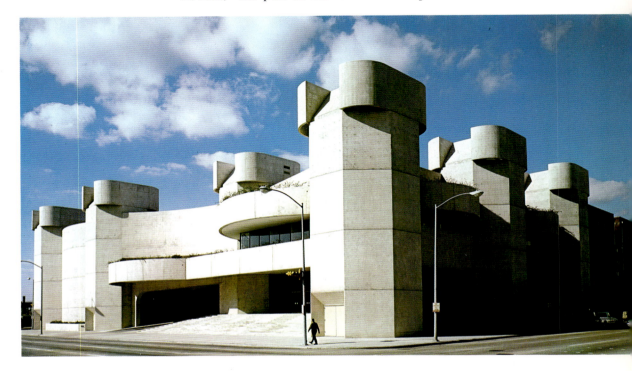

Houston's Alley Theatre, a monument of modern architecture

the longtime enemy cities of Fort Worth and Dallas to bury the hatchet. To counter Houston's spectacular growth and its dramatic emergence, thanks to NASA and the Astronauts, as one of the best known, internationally, of American cities, Dallas and Fort Worth have turned partners to dream up a project that promises in the economic sphere to be as "breathtaking" as Fort Worth's Kay Kimbell Museum. This will be simply the "biggest and best" International Airport in the whole wide world, as large when the last phase is completed as Manhattan Island itself. This much-vaunted collective enterprise is designed to make the Dallas-Fort Worth area the veritable "hub" of the world of air transportation, the gateway to international exchange. It will undoubtedly for a time at least remain the most modern and the most complete air service facility in existence.

Texans stress again and again the theme of the unity of the state. How strange it is that no political party has ever tried to profit from the extraordinary privilege granted Texas on annexation, the right to split into five states when its population justified. There is no question that the population is now large enough; Texas is fifth in population in the country. Its size alone would justify a change that would give the present Texas area ten Senators instead of two. Why not? As has often been pointed out, if you could hinge the borders of Texas and fold them over, the southernmost point, Brownsville, would be only a hundred or so miles from the Canadian border; East Texas would reach the Pacific Ocean; El Paso—which is halfway between Houston and Los Angeles—would fold across to stick out into the Atantic Ocean.

Not to cash in on this option is all the more surprising when one reflects on the vast diversity of the geographical areas of Texas. East Texas, or a good part of it, is called "The Piney Woods" because it is the westernmost reach of the great Southern pine forests, originating in Virginia and North Carolina. It is a green land, Old South in tradition and life-style, and it has the largest Negro population of any area in the state. And in the Big Thicket, it has one of the most interesting wilderness areas in the nation, one that even contains an Indian Reservation, that of the Alabama-Coushatta tribe. By contrast, faraway along the Rio Grande in West Texas, the magnificent Big Bend

The Rio Grande

National Park is a brown land, very sparsely inhabited, rich in landscape rather than in oil fields. At the western edge of the Piney Woods, the waxy "Blacklands"—so fertile for cotton—run from the Oklahoma border on down through Dallas and Waco and the Brazos River Bottomlands. To the west of Dallas, beginning as we have seen at Fort Worth, is "West Texas" extending all the way to the New Mexico border, but separate from the Texas Panhandle in the northern reaches of the state, and really separate from the Latin flavor of West Texas' last outpost, the mountain country around El Paso, the foothills of the Rockies. In the center of the state lies the special LBJ "Hill Country," whose hills project wonderful configurations against the deep blue sky. At its southern edge lies what many consider the most interesting triangle in Texas, the land along the Gulf of Mexico, inland from Houston on a line to San Antonio and from that quaint and picturesque city, the "Venice of Texas," with its beautiful downtown waterway, on southwest to Del Rio, on the Mexican border—a land of subtropical charm, amazing springs, rich soil that yields four crops a year. And then there is the rapidly developing "Texas Riviera," from Corpus Christi midway along the Texas Gulf Coast on down the hundred-mile length of Padre Island to Brownsville and the citrus-rich Rio Grande semi-tropical valley. Eighty miles of the thin and narrow but very long stringbean Padre Island have been reserved as a National Seashore. Meantime, private property owners on both northern and southern tips of the island confidently expect to duplicate the Florida land boom soon. All this "Magic Valley" area benefits from an ever-growing wintertime population of northerners and midwesterners seeking the sun. Many Texans are unaware of the beauty of this area. This may be due to the fact that most of the excitement in Texas at the moment seems to originate in the big cities, but as the cities grow increasingly sophisticated, it is likely that Texans will reassert their need to live outdoors, to return to the natural, to the land. Texas will remain a largely vacant dizzying expanse of space, a vacant land populated with more and more small oases. It now has ten million people and that many cows. For a long time to come, this ratio will probably prevail, and continue to give to diverse and contradictory Texas its unifying "western" life-style.

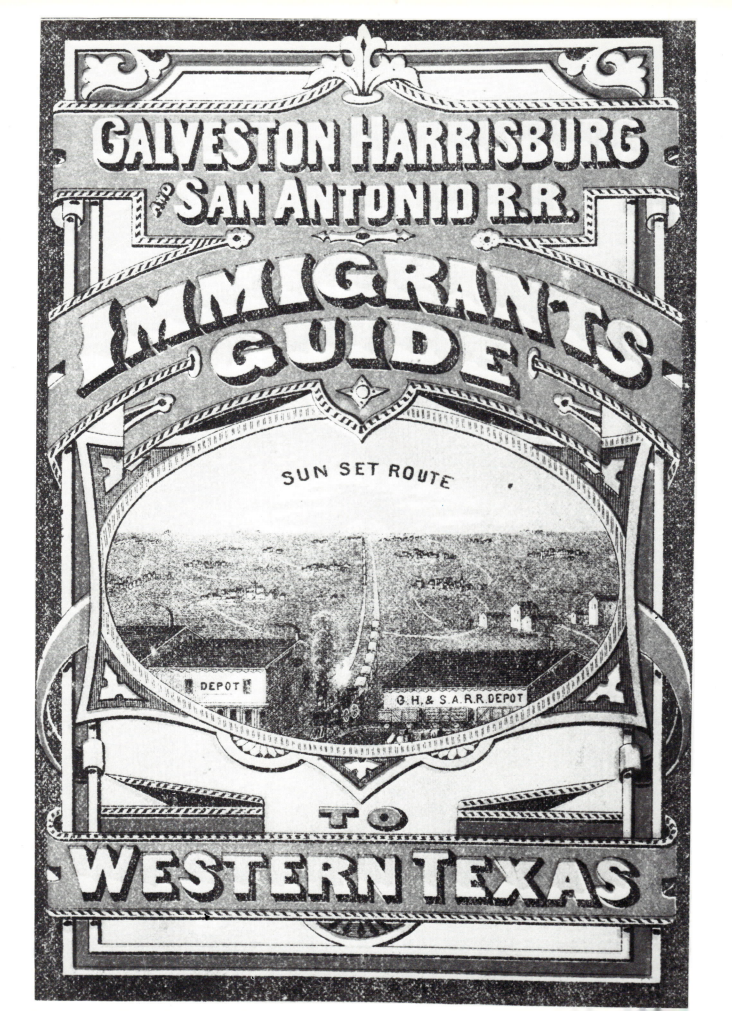

THE CREATION OF TEXAS

The empty plains of Texas contained only a scattering of Indians when the Spanish explorer Cabeza de Vaca was shipwrecked on the coast near Galveston in the year 1528. More than a century and a half elapsed before the Spaniards established control of the vast region, and even then they sent in settlers only because they were worried that the land would be taken over by the French. Over the next 150 years a mixed population of Anglo-Americans, Mexican-Americans, and black slaves moved in, but by the time Texas became independent in 1836 the population was still only around 30,000, approximately one person for every 5,000 acres. Since that time the population has grown to more than 10 million. The following pages survey the story of the state's growth—in its history and in its tradition, in its economy, and above all, in its people who have always been Texas's greatest wealth.

Opposite: The cover of a railroad guidebook touting the attractions of western Texas.

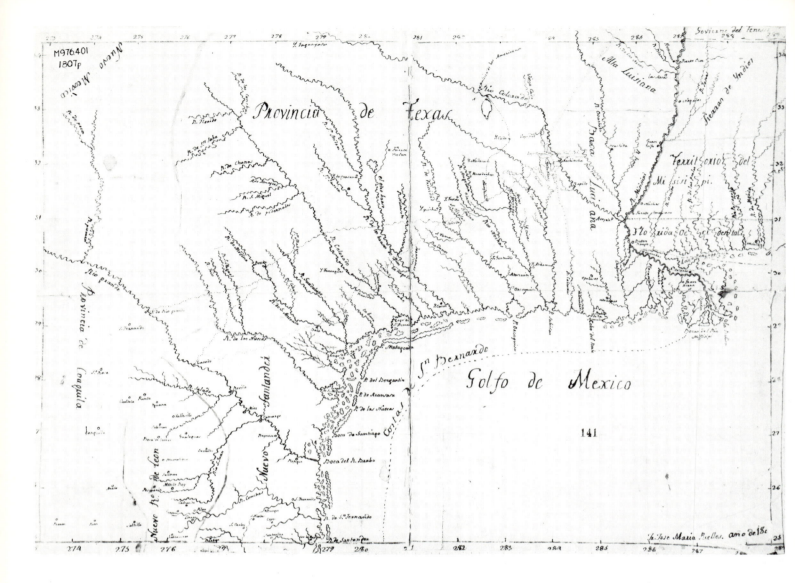

Right: The title page of the first book about Texas, Cabeza de Vaca's *Relacións*, displays the coat of arms of the author. *Above:* A Spanish map dating from around 1810 shows the region of Texas. *Opposite:* French settlers at Champs d'Asile in 1818.

Throughout much of the seventeenth and eighteenth centuries Texas remained a neglected outpost of Spain's vastly wealthy Mexican domain, despite a scattering of mission-centered settlements that kept a tenuous hold on the country. There had been various attempts by the French to settle the country from their neighboring colony of Louisiana, but generally both powers agreed that the empty plains of Texas were hardly worth the effort of colonization. It was not until the European powers surrendered their hold and new nations born on the American continent—Mexico and the United States—began expanding that Texas attracted serious interest.

Top: An 1885 view of the battle of the Alamo, where almost 200 heroic Texans met death rather than surrender to the Mexicans. *Bottom:* Heroes of the Texas revolution. *Left to right:* Sam Houston, commander of the Texas armies; Jim Bowie, who died at the Alamo; Juan Seguin, who served in Houston's army and later became mayor of San Antonio; Davy Crockett, whose name was already legendary on the frontier, before his arrival at the Alamo.

Americans first came to Texas in a group, by invitation, under the leadership of Stephen Austin, each settler promising to become a citizen of Mexico and swear allegiance to the Catholic faith. By 1830 there were almost 20,000 Texans—the vast majority of them English-speaking. In that year, Mexico, disturbed by the fact that Americans were coming to dominate the region, clamped down on further immigration. The United States offered to purchase Texas, but the offer was turned down. Eventually as Texans grew more and more resentful of Mexican control, an open breach developed. The breach, though patched over, was never healed, and the instability of the Mexican government, tossed this way and that by frequent revolutions, gave Texans a chance to slip away. By 1836 Texas had gained its independence after a fierce war marked by battles and massacres—at the Alamo, Goliad, San Jacinto—names that have become part of both Texas and American legend.

Left: Frederick Remington's famous "Cowboy." *Opposite, top:* In 1847 the signing of a treaty between German settlers and Comanche Indians gave the Germans title to the lands around Fredericksburg near Austin. *Opposite, bottom:* A Lone Star Flag flies over the Texas capitol building at Austin, a rough pioneer structure built in 1839.

Overleaf: The cattle-shipping town of Abilene soon after the Civil War.

The independent republic of Texas with its capital at Austin quickly made its mark on the world stage. France established a legation at Austin, and England also began to court the young republic. For almost ten years after independence in 1836 Texans waged a cold war with their former rulers, the Mexicans, a war that often reached boiling point. Another war took place with the Indians on the Texas frontier, a war that did not end until the United States built a string of army forts along Texas's western frontier. By the time the Indians were finally pacified Texas had been in and out of the Union: being annexed in 1845 after a prolonged political campaign, seceding in 1861, and then being brought back into the Union by the victorious northern armies after the Civil War. By the time the Civil War was over, western Texas had become a cattle kingdom with vast spreads and roaring cowtowns and that Texas folk hero the cowboy, whose exploits made the name of Texas famous all over the world.

Top: An Indian woman on the Alabama-Coushatta reservation. *Opposite, top:* A Polish wedding party. *Bottom, left to right:* Jacob de Cordova, a Jew and the first mayor of Waco; Prince Carl Solms-Braunfels, who sponsored German immigration; two Greek sisters—the woman on the left emigrated to Dallas, the one on the right remained in Greece.

The most prominent Texas Indian tribes were the Caddoes of the east and the Comanches, Lipan Apaches, and Coahuiltecan tribes of central and west Texas; later the Cherokees migrated into the state. Now Indians survive as a group only on one east Texas reservation inhabited by just a small percentage of the state's almost 20,000 Texas Indians. The German influence was very strong in early Texas and many hill-country towns still maintain German customs. Poles settled in the countryside east of San Antonio in 1854, and their town of Panna Maria is reputed to be the oldest Polish settlement in America. A smattering of Jews came to Texas in the nineteenth century, and now Jewish communities flourish in the major cities. Greek and Lebanese immigrants also came, making the Texas cities a mixture of many ethnic strains.

Opposite: Leadbelly, Huddie Ledbetter, the great blues singer. *Above:* The post office at Norse Texas, established by Norwegian immigrants.

In the nineteenth century, Alsatians came from Europe to settle Castroville in the hill country. Near Beaumont Dutch immigrants founded the town of Nederland, naming it after their homeland. Czechs settled on the blacklands of Lavaca County, and Norwegians established a colony along the Bosque River south of Fort Worth. Blacks had long been settled in eastern Texas, most of them descendants of plantation slaves who had been brought by their owners from the East. Now one in every ten Texans is black. Most Texas blacks still live in eastern Texas in or around the major cities, particularly Houston. In the period since World War II the black community has made impressive gains both socially and economically, though some inequities still remain.

White Protestants, whose ancestors came from the British Isles, make up the most important population group in Texas. They dominate the state and give Texas culture much of its distinctive flavor. Most of their forebears arrived from the other American states, but some came directly from the Old World. Ties with Scotland, for instance, have always been strong; a good deal of the money backing the expansion of the cattle ranches came from Scottish financiers. The second greatest ethnic group in the state is Mexican-American. One in five Texas school-children speaks Spanish as a native tongue. Some cities, such as San Antonio and El Paso, are as Mexican in flavor as they are Anglo-American. Texas is a border state, and it partakes of two cultures which merge to form a uniquely Texan blend.

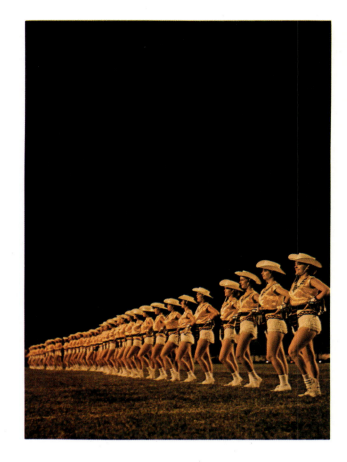

Above, left: Scottish stoneworkers building the State Capitol at Austin. *Left:* Mexican-American children in costume at Brownsville. *Above:* A marching team of college girls performing at the Cotton Bowl during the State Fair.

43

Traditionally, Texas's wealth has been based on three sources: cotton, cattle, and oil. Cotton was the earliest; in the 1830's Southern plantation owners moved into east Texas and planted cotton fields. Now cotton is grown on irrigated lands in the western part of the state too, and it remains Texas's most valuable field crop. Raising cattle is the most important agricultural operation in the state, as it has been for decades. Texas contains more than one-tenth of all the cattle in the United States. The greatest contribution to the state's economy in this decade has been made by oil and natural gas and by the petrochemical industry based on them. From the time that the Spindletop gusher erupted near Beaumont in 1901 until now, production has increased immensely. Enormous wealth has come from beneath the soil, enriching not just the oil barons, but the entire state.

Opposite: Hereford cattle. Above: A wheatfield north of Amarillo in the Panhandle. Right: Spindletop. Below: A cotton gin in the blacklands town of Granger, north of Austin.

A PICTURE TOUR

The more than a quarter million square miles that comprise the vast domain of Texas present an immensely varied landscape, from the mountainous barrens of the far west to the pine woods of the east, from the windswept plains of the Panhandle to the palmgroves of the subtropical Rio Grande Valley. On the following pages is a picture tour of that imperial domain, displaying its remarkable diversity and its great beauty. It begins in the pine woods along the Sabine River, and follows a route that goes south along the coast, down to the Mexican border, and then crosses the state again, up through the hill country and prairies of central Texas to the Panhandle, to end finally in the spectacular desert and mountain country of Texas's far west.

Opposite: Cowboys and sheep on a West Texas ranch

Overleaf: An old-fashioned, water-driven gristmill still grinds corn near the town of Poynor in East Texas's Henderson County.

The century-old city of Atlanta, in Texas's northeast corner, was settled by Georgians and many of its houses still reflect the Old South, like the pillared mansion *above*. The old Nacogdoches University building, *right*, dates from the 1850's. A few miles west of Atlanta lies Daingerfield Lake, *opposite,* with its population of ducks.

A vast pine and hardwood forest, known as the Piney Woods, covers some 16 million acres in East Texas, making lumbering one of the region's major industries. *Above:* An East Texas sawmill. *Opposite:* The Sabine National Forest, seen from a lookout tower. At the southern reaches of the Piney Woods is the Big Thicket, *below,* an almost impenetrable region of streams, marshes, and woods.

A causeway, *below,* carries a highway across Steinhagen Lake, near the Louisiana border, one of the more than 150 major artificial reservoirs built in the state since 1900. *Opposite:* an older form of transportation, a riverboat on Big Cypress Bayou in the historic old northeast Texas river port of Jefferson.

Caddo Lake, *opposite,* astride the Louisiana border, is difficult to navigate because of the tangled vegetation floating on its surface. *Above:* A rose field near Canton. In northeastern Texas more than fifteen million rose bushes are grown for sale annually.

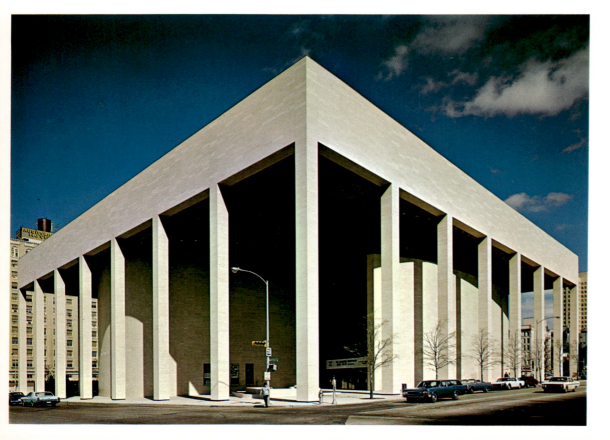

The largest city in Texas and in the entire South, Houston is also one of the country's major seaports. Its skyline appears *above*. *Left* and *below:* The Sam Houston Monument and the fountains at the entrance to Hermann Park, both illuminated at night. *Opposite page:* One of Texas's major cultural attractions, the Jesse H. Jones Hall for the Performing Arts.

A stadium unique as the Colosseum in Rome, Houston's famous Astrodome, *opposite*, can be used for baseball or football. *Below:* The exterior.

In the Houston area: *Above*, a petrochemical plant at Pasadena. *Below*, N.A.S.A.'s Manned Spacecraft Center on the outskirts of the city. *Opposite*, a rice field. Rice is one of Texas's most valuable crops.

Galveston's historic Bishop's Palace, *opposite,* contains a treasure trove of Victorian art. Across from Galveston Island lies the sandy Bolivar Peninsula, with its lighthouse and fishing shacks, *above.*

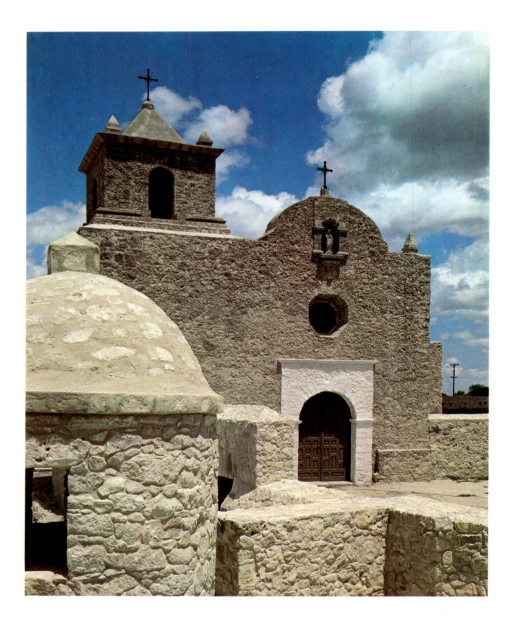

Two monuments of Texas's war for independence: *Above,* Presidio la Bahia at Goliad, the old Spanish fort where almost 350 Texas soldiers were massacred by the Mexicans in 1836, although they had already surrendered. *Opposite,* the San Jacinto monument, on the outskirts of Houston, marks the site of a battle where the Texans resoundingly defeated the Mexican army to win their independence.

One of Texas's largest cities, Corpus Christi, is both a resort and an industrial center. *Above:* An aerial view showing the marinas and curved breakwater lying off the city's center. *Opposite:* The marina docks.

Outside Corpus Christi, the shifting dunes of Padre Island National Seashore stretch over 80 miles along one of the barrier islands that guard almost the entire length of the Texas coast. *Below:* The National Park Service pavilion for visitors. *Opposite:* Sea oats and morning glory on the unspoiled dunes.

Port Isabel, a few miles above the Mexican border, is the access point for the south end of Padre Island and well known as a fishing port. *Below:* The town's docks. *Opposite:* The Port Isabel lighthouse.

Agriculture dominates the economy of Texas's far south, but fishing is important too. *Above:* Shrimp boats at Port Aransas near Corpus Christi. *Opposite:* A vast plantation of citrus groves in the Rio Grande Valley.

Above: The winding Rio Grande near Brownsville. *Opposite:* A cabbage field in the Rio Grande Valley, boasting a Texas-size crop.

San Antonio is Texas's greatest center of Hispanic culture. *Above,* is one of the city's many missions, Nuestra Senora de la Purisma Concepción, completed in 1755. *Opposite,* two contemporary buildings: The Hall of Performing Arts, with its Mexican-style mosaic mural, and the HemisFair Tower, well known as a symbol of the city.

Overleaf: A coat of green covers the knobby hills of the Texas hill country, whose dude ranches and lakes make it one of the state's prime tourist areas. These hills lie a few miles north of San Antonio.

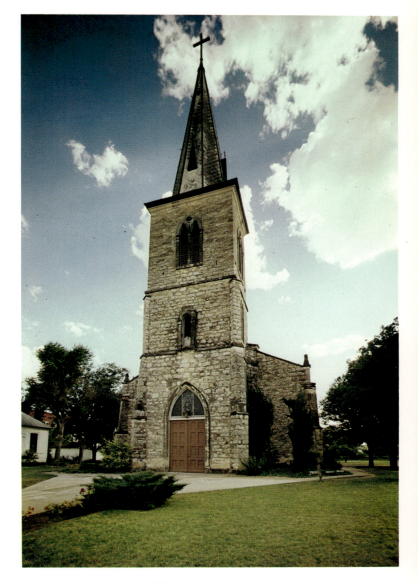

A reconstructed octagonal church, *opposite*, in Fredericksburg, west of Austin, houses mementos of the Germans who first settled the town. The ranch home of the late Lyndon B. Johnson, *below*, lies a few miles outside Fredericksburg. Castroville, near San Antonio, was settled by Alsatian immigrants who built St. Louis Church, *right*, out of stone in 1869.

Lily pads float on the surface of the San Marcos River which flows down from the hill country to join the Guadalupe at the coastal plain town of Gonzales.

Austin boasts the nation's largest state capitol. The building, *opposite,* was built of pink granite in the 1880's by a group of Chicago businessmen, in exchange for a grant of 3 million acres of state land in the Panhandle. *Above:* The interior of the dome. *Left:* Austin's colonnaded governor's mansion constructed in 1856.

A 27-story tower, *above,* dominates the campus of the South's largest university, The University of Texas at Austin. *Opposite* are two other Austin monuments: *Top,* the house in which the writer O. Henry lived from 1885 to 1895; *bottom,* the French Legation which was constructed in 1841 by the King of France's Minister to the Republic of Texas.

Northwest of Austin, impoundments have formed a series of lakes along the central reaches of the 600-mile-long Colorado, one of the major rivers of Texas. *Below:* Lake LBJ. *Opposite:* Hamilton Pool, a swimming area on the river.

Sixty-five miles of the Colorado's course form Lake Travis, an important boating center. *Opposite:* A regatta on the lake. A few miles from the lake's eastern shore lie the Inner Space Caverns at Georgetown, *above,* discovered only in the 1960's.

Halfway between Austin and Houston lies the pastoral landscape of Washington County. *Opposite:* Bluebonnets edging a pasture near Brenham. *Below:* A monument a few miles away at La Grange, commemorating a group of Texas soldiers massacred by the Mexicans in 1842.

In the old town of Salado, south of Waco, the waters of Salado Creek provided power for a nineteenth-century grain mill.

More Texas acreage is devoted to grain sorghum than to any other crop. The field *below* is near Salado. A few miles north is Waco's historic Fort Fisher *(opposite, bottom)* where a Texas Ranger fort was established in 1837. The old Stagecoach Inn at Round Top, east of Austin, is now a museum devoted to the immigrant groups who populated Texas *(opposite, top)*.

At Dinosaur Valley State Park in Glen Rose, south of Fort Worth, rocks imprinted with dinosaur footprints are scattered along the course of the Paluxy River, *right. Above:* One of the statues in the State Park, a replica of an early Texas inhabitant, *tyrannosaurus rex.* Old Fort Parker, *opposite,* in Groesbeck east of Waco, is the site of a famous Indian raid which took place in 1836.

Three of Texas's many ornate courthouses. *Above:* At Hillsboro in Hill County, an extravagant confection of various architectural influences including a French mansard roof and classical pillars. *Opposite, top:* At Stephenville in Erath County, a building in the Romanesque style. *Opposite, bottom:* At La Grange in Fayette County, a fortress-like structure that faintly evokes a Gothic castle.

Above: The Fort Worth skyline, with Christmas lights illuminating the city's skyscrapers. *Opposite:* The immense convention center at Fort Worth, covering fourteen city blocks.

Opposite: The skyscrapers of Dallas. *Above:* The Dallas Theatre Center, designed by Frank Lloyd Wright. *Top:* The John F. Kennedy Memorial, designed by Philip Johnson and built near the site where President Kennedy was assassinated.

Denison, just south of the Oklahoma border, is an important railroad junction. Dwight Eisenhower, whose father worked in the Denison railway shops, was born in 1890 in the white frame house *opposite. Above:* the courthouse at Denton, a town that boasts two universities.

Above: Rock and eroded red soil northwest of Seymour. *Opposite, top:* Snow blanketing the ground at Wichita Falls. *Opposite, bottom:* Four inhabitants of a prairie dog town on the High Plains.

A horse remuda at a ranch in King County (area almost 1,000 square miles; population almost 500). *Opposite and below:* Cowboys select their horses from a herd. *Opposite, bottom:* Lunch.

Within Palo Duro Canyon, *opposite,* red canyon walls tower above the valley floor. *Above:* A great flint rock in Alibates Flint Quarries National Monument, north of Amarillo.

Overleaf: Palo Duro Canyon in the Panhandle was carved out of the High Plains over millenniums.

On the Texas plains: *Opposite:* Hereford cattle on a ranch in the Panhandle. *Below:* An aerial view of cattle grazing near a watering tank.

At top: Historic Fort Phantom Hill, north of Abilene. *Above:* The museum at the Midland-Odessa airport enshrining the first plane built in Texas. *Opposite:* Lubbock's Texas Tech University.

Below: San Angelo's Fort Concho, the best preserved of all Texas frontier forts. *Opposite:* Lake Nasworthy, one of several major reservoirs that surround San Angelo.

Two major tourist sites of the hill country: The canyons of the Frio River, *above*, and the spectacularly beautiful rock formations of the Caverns of Sonora, *opposite*.

Post office, gas station, and general store, the Telegraph Store *opposite* is the social and economic center of the tiny town of Telegraph in the sheep-ranching county of Kimble, west of San Antonio. The dead hawk over the gate on a ranch at Del Rio on the Rio Grande, *left,* was hung there as a warning to other hawks; the skull affixed to the side of a log cabin, *above,* in Kerr County in the hill country is for decorative purposes only.

Fort McKavett, *opposite,* and Fort Clark, *above,* were part of a string of forts defending Texas's western settlements against Indians. McKavett is just south of San Angelo. Clark lies further south, near the Rio Grande. The region is a major sheep raising center. *Below, left:* A statue of Popeye in the town square at Crystal City, near the Rio Grande, in a district noted for growing spinach. *Below, right:* Angora kids at a watering tank.

Above, The Pecos River brings a touch of green to the barren West Texas landscape. *Opposite:* The Rio Grande flows through Santa Elena Canyon in Big Bend National Park.

Opposite: A rock formation in Big Bend National Park, with the mountains of Mexico in the distance. *Above and overleaf:* The Rio Grande.

Opposite: The ruins of an adobe house stand beside a butte in Big Bend National Park. *Above:* In the Big Bend country, two vultures, perched on a dead tree, spread their wings.

Overleaf: The rugged and almost roadless Chinati Mountains of Presidio County border the Rio Grande.

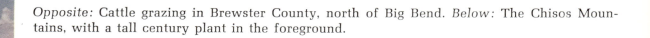

Opposite: Cattle grazing in Brewster County, north of Big Bend. *Below:* The Chisos Mountains, with a tall century plant in the foreground.

Ruined Fort Leaton, *opposite*, almost three centuries old, was once a Spanish mission and a pioneer trading post. The dunes of Monahans Sandhills State Park, *below*, cover thousands of acres.

A stand of spiny giant yucca plants in Hudspeth County.

Above: A sheep ranch near Marathon. *Opposite, top:* Indian pictographs at Hueco Tanks State Park in El Paso County. *Opposite, bottom:* A jackrabbit, one of the most common of Texas's animals.

Overleaf: The ruins of an old stage-coach-stop on the road to El Paso near Pine Springs, a few miles south of the New Mexico border.

148

Guadaloupe Mountain National Park contains Texas's highest mountains. *Opposite and above:* Two views in the Park's McKittrick Canyon.

Overleaf: A cotton field near Van Horn, on an immense mountain-ringed plain devoted to irrigated farming.

An old cemetery and a railroad trestle lie in the valley of El Paso del Norte, *below,* where the Spaniards first settled the land that became Texas. *Opposite:* A thirty-three-foot-high statue of Christ overlooking El Paso atop Sierra del Cristo Rey.

An aerial tramway *(left)* lifts visitors to the top of Ranger Peak almost 6,000 feet above El Paso. *Below:* A mountaintop view of the city.

Overleaf: The state's oldest mission is at Ysleta, near El Paso. Ysleta was the first community established by Europeans on Texas soil.